TAKE YOUR LIFE BACK
WORKBOOK

TAKE YOUR LIFE BACK

WORKBOOK

*Five Sessions to Transform
Your Relationships with God,
Yourself, and Others*

STEPHEN ARTERBURN, M.Ed.
DAVID STOOP, Ph.D.
with Margot Starbuck

**TYNDALE®
MOMENTUM**

*An Imprint of
Tyndale House Publishers, Inc.*

Visit Tyndale online at www.tyndale.com.

Visit Tyndale Momentum online at www.tyndalemomentum.com.

Tyndale Momentum and the Tyndale Momentum logo are registered trademarks of Tyndale House Publishers, Inc. Tyndale Momentum is an imprint of Tyndale House Publishers, Inc.

Take Your Life Back Workbook: Five Sessions to Transform Your Relationships with God, Yourself, and Others

Designed by Ron Kaufmann

The authors are represented by the literary agency of WordServe Literary Group, www.wordserveliterary.com.

Scripture quotations are taken from the *Holy Bible*, New Living Translation, copyright © 1996, 2004, 2015 by Tyndale House Foundation. Used by permission of Tyndale House Publishers, Inc., Carol Stream, Illinois 60188. All rights reserved.

Printed in the United States of America

22   21   20   19   18   17   16
7   6   5   4   3   2   1

CONTENTS

Questions You May Be Asking

Who should use this study?

If you feel as if something, or someone, has a hold on your life and you're ready to be free, the *Take Your Life Back Workbook* was written for you.

Perhaps you've experienced a power that overwhelms your best intentions to live the life that God intends for you. Maybe it feels as if there's a force inside you that sabotages your best efforts and frustrates your deepest desires. You've seen the way it meddles with your relationships, and you'd like to live differently.

Maybe you've experienced trauma in the past—from physical, emotional, sexual, or spiritual abuse, or from neglect or abandonment—which has left its mark on your life through depression, shame, addiction, or dependency. As you read through *Take Your Life Back*, this companion piece can help you rediscover hope and give you a vision and a plan for taking your life back.

If you feel stuck, as if something other than you is controlling your life, the *Take Your Life Back Workbook* can help set you free.

Should I approach the *Take Your Life Back Workbook* individually or with a group?

There are great reasons to study the *Take Your Life Back Workbook* in a group setting, and also important reasons for studying it on your own.

Here's why you might choose to study the *Take Your Life Back Workbook* in a group:

> » Group study offers the supportive presence of a community that cares for you.
> » Group study gives you the opportunity to lend care and encouragement to others who are also on the journey.
> » Hearing the stories of others may shed light on your own life experience.
> » Sharing your story in the presence of those who care can break the power of lingering toxic shame.

Here's why you might choose to study the *Take Your Life Back Workbook* individually:

» Individual study provides the safety to return to the most difficult parts of your past that you might not be prepared to share with others.

» You can explore the uniqueness of your personal story at your own pace.

» When you encounter a particularly painful moment in your story, you can pause to offer it to God and listen for God's compassionate response.

Because there are such compelling reasons for journeying together with a group and also for exploring your story individually, this workbook has been designed to offer opportunities for both.

In each session, we have designated which conversations are meant to be shared with a group and which are for private reflection. As the people in your group begin to know and care for one another, they may choose to share the more sensitive parts of their stories, but no one is ever *obligated* to share.

How do I access and use the free companion videos by Stephen Arterburn and David Stoop that go along with this workbook?

The videos can be found online at **www.takeyourlifeback.tv**. Watch these together with reading *Take Your Life Back* to prepare for taking part in group discussions and completing the workbook.

Clarity, honesty, trust, security
(Knowing)
him

Tips to Get the Most from

This Workbook

Guard Your Privacy
Consider this workbook to be as sacred as a personal diary—for your eyes only. These pages are where you can feel free to record your innermost thoughts and what you are learning along the way. Be sure to keep your workbook in a secure place.

Mark It Up!
As you work through this guide, some words or phrases may grab your heart in a new way. Don't be afraid to circle or highlight them or draw little symbols in the margins—whatever works best for you to remember the key concepts and truths. In the margin next to each fresh insight, consider jotting down the date and a brief note to remind yourself what you have seen with new eyes. These are the trail markers that will help you later retrace the journey you traveled, with God's help, to take your life back.

Watch the Videos

After you've read the chapters of *Take Your Life Back* for each session, take advantage of the introductory videos that Stephen Arterburn and David Stoop have created. These can be found online at **www.takeyourlifeback.tv**. Watching the videos is a good way to transition from the book into your workbook session as you begin to think through and discuss the ideas and principles you're learning.

Come Prepared

Before each group meeting, be sure to do the assigned reading and complete the corresponding portion of the workbook. The better prepared you are for each meeting, the more you are likely to contribute to and benefit from the group discussions. Working through the Questions for Personal Reflection will help you go deeper into each section of *Take Your Life Back*.

Road Map for the Journey

HERE'S A GLIMPSE at the road ahead. When your group decides on a meeting schedule, jot the dates below the title of each session to remind you which material to study in advance.

Part I: The Reactive Life
Session 1: Understanding the Reactive Life
Date of group meeting: _____

Before the meeting: Read the Introduction and chapters 1–3 in *Take Your Life Back*.

Session 2: Roots of Reactive Living
Date of group meeting: _____

Before the meeting: Read chapters 4–6 in *Take Your Life Back*.

Session 3: Shame, Trauma, and Losing Yourself
Date of meeting: _____

Before the meeting: Read chapters 7–10 in *Take Your Life Back*.

Part II: The Responsive Life

Session 4: Taking Your Life Back

Date of meeting: _____

Before the meeting: Read the Reintroduction and chapters 11–12 in *Take Your Life Back*.

Session 5: Health on the Journey

Date of meeting: _____

Before the meeting: Read chapters 13–14 in *Take Your Life Back*.

A Note from the Authors

SOMETHING IN YOUR life owns you, and you're ready for a change.

Maybe it's a trauma from your past—emotional, physical, or sexual—that continues to exert influence in your life today.

Maybe it's an addiction.

Or a relationship with someone who was, or is, addicted.

Perhaps it's a current obsession.

Or maybe you're living with the fallout from a season when you made some poor choices.

Perhaps your parents weren't able to offer all that you needed—and deserved—in order to thrive.

Whatever the source of your dependency, you feel as if an external force has taken control of your life. You live with the lasting effects of unresolved wounds that interfere with your daily living. You feel caught in the grip of something beyond yourself.

You've been living *reactively* instead of *responsively*.

Though reactive living takes many forms, it is often rooted in a lack of healthy attachments in our earliest years when we didn't bond well with our caregivers. Consequently, our impulse is to *react*—often with defensiveness, projection, blame, or shame—rather than *respond* in healthy ways.

You're ready to live differently, but until now you haven't known how.

Today you have the opportunity to take your life back.

If you're like a lot of people, you may have resisted walking the path toward redemption—until now—for fear of what it will mean for those around you.

If I'm honest about my past, you may be thinking, *it could rupture my relationships.* We understand. But this journey isn't about blaming those who came before you. It's about noticing what really happened and learning to walk in new ways.

If you're tired of living in reaction to negative power and destructive control in your life, this guide, as a companion to our book *Take Your Life Back*, can help you live the life you were meant to live. In these pages, we'll help you apply what you've learned in *Take Your Life Back* so that you can take charge of your past and your current circumstances, and you can look forward to the road ahead.

The reason we wrote *Take Your Life Back* was to show you that real and lasting change *is* possible. Not only *possible*, but also *achievable*. At some point, we all must stop *reacting* and learn how to *respond* appropriately. If your life has been hijacked, it's up to you to take it back.

Transformation won't happen just because you've been inspired by thoughts or ideas. Real change happens as you take it to the next level by doing the work of exploring what has kept you bound up. We've designed this workbook as a tool to help you gain traction in your life by applying what you've learned to your unique situation. As you do, and as you *choose* to live differently, we believe that—with God's help—you will discover and walk in new freedom.

When you first make the choice to get better, it may feel uncomfortable. If you've felt that you've been without options or that healthy living is out of reach for you, you may even believe that change isn't possible. But it is.

Every person's journey looks different, and yours begins where you are right now. If you're willing to take one step at a time, we will help you learn how to

» see your struggle from a different perspective,
» eliminate whatever destructive force or influence has hold of your life, and
» experience change that sets you free.

We not only believe that God's good purpose for you includes hope, meaning, and transformation, but we believe that you have what it takes to grab hold of all three. We have held you in our hearts as we've prayed over and written this book, and today we are cheering you on as you choose to do the *good*, hard work of taking your life back.

Stephen Arterburn
David Stoop

SESSION 1:

UNDERSTANDING THE REACTIVE LIFE

Date of group meeting:

_____

BEFORE YOUR GROUP MEETING: Read the Introduction and chapters 1–3 in *Take Your Life Back*.

Take to your group meeting:
1. *Take Your Life Back*
2. *Take Your Life Back Workbook*
3. journal (optional)
4. pen/pencil

Introduction
We'll begin this session by pausing to notice where we are and where we've been. In the introduction to *Take Your Life*

Back, Stephen Arterburn describes a force inside him that controlled everything in his life. It disabled him emotionally and wreaked havoc in his relationships. David Stoop drank and acted out throughout high school, so he also knows what it's like to have been far from God. If you've ever been in the pit, Steve and Dave know a bit about what your life has been like.

Both have dealt with deep-seated shame and have known the joy of taking their lives back by returning to the Father. David explains: "When I turned back to God, there was no shame or condemnation—only the open arms of God the Father welcoming me back." Our hope is that you will keep your eyes on that open-armed welcome and that God's acceptance of you will embolden you to do the necessary work to take your life back. This journey takes *courage*, but you are not traveling alone.

Although in the past you weren't able to change your circumstances, you can today. In fact, we're confident that meaningful change is possible and you can experience new life as you bravely face the past.

This week, we're looking at a story that Jesus told, which has come to be known as the parable of the prodigal son (Luke 15:11-32)—though Steve and David observe that it might just as easily be called the parable of the father's love or the parable of the angry brother. We'll also look at Rembrandt's masterpiece *The Return of the Prodigal Son*, which is based on the same story. Both the parable and the painting depict a father who is quick to forgive and embrace those who turn to him. As we approach the group discussion, remember that the Holy Spirit will empower and embolden you as you bravely face the past and look forward to a different future.

Group Discussion

Opening Prayer

Father, you have made yourself known as one who welcomes those of us who have lost our way. We surrender ourselves to your Holy Spirit to guide our time together and grant us courage and wisdom to take our lives back. We trust that you are able to do all things according to your own purpose. Amen.

Scripture Focus

Read aloud the story of the two sons who have lost control of their lives in Luke 15:11-32. If group members are using different Bible translations, take note of any meaningful differences between translations. Do these differences offer additional insight?

Conversation Starter

Use Google Images (https://images.google.com) or another source to look at Rembrandt's painting *The Return of the Prodigal Son.* How does Rembrandt's interpretation of the parable compare to the account in the Gospel of Luke? What parts of the story come to life, and what differences do you see?

Discussion

1. A central part of taking your life back is returning to the Father who loves you. As you think about the story that Jesus tells, how easy or difficult is it for you to see, with the eyes of your heart, the face of a gracious Father tipped

in your direction—a loving Father with arms open wide to embrace you exactly as you are and not as you "should be"? Why is it difficult, or not so difficult, for you to believe that God the Father is gracious?

2. Both the elder son and the younger son surrendered their lives to forces outside of themselves. The younger son "acted out" with wild living, and the elder son "acted in," filling his heart with disappointment, resentment, and judgment. Which of the two brothers do you most closely identify with, and why?

- *If you connected most with the humbled son who has returned . . .*

   The wayward younger son acts out by leaving home and living as he pleases. Yet, one day he wakes up cold and hungry, thinking about the warm, well-fed servants back home. Rather than being motivated by authentic repentance, he's driven home by hunger and poverty.

What signals tell you that you're stuck? What red flags have alerted you to the reality that you are owned by something outside of—or inside—yourself? In a nutshell: What parts of your life are not working?

- *If you connected most with the elder son who stayed home . . .*

The elder son feels disappointed, frustrated, jealous, and possibly even abandoned. Far from having ownership of his own life, he lives in bondage to disillusionment and a sense of entitlement. He needs to take his life back as much as his brother does.

What signals tell you that you're stuck? What red flags have alerted you to the reality that you are owned by something outside of—or inside—yourself? In a nutshell: What parts of your life are not working?

3. Those seeking to recover from classic dependency must understand their childhood relationships to discover how their real self was lost. Those seeking to recover from secondary codependency must understand their adult relationships. Which of the following symptoms of classic dependency feel familiar to you?

☐ I worry about being seen as selfish or controlling.
☐ I worry about whether I am liked by others.
☐ I seek to keep the peace, even at my own expense.
☐ I monitor the moods of others.
☐ I can be too trusting of others.
☐ I make excuses for the behavior of other people.
☐ I sacrifice readily for others, but not for myself.

We gain the most traction in taking back our lives when we can identify the real ways in which our dependency is hurting us and others.

If you checked any of the boxes above, share with the group a recent example from your life.

Where in the story of your childhood do you believe this dependency might be rooted?

4. Perhaps you were affected by secondary dependency and are now in an unhealthy relationship. If there was no serious abuse during your childhood, you may have been wounded through trauma or difficult relationships. Perhaps there was a shaming or guilt-inducing incident that rocked the core of your self-image. Or maybe a more recent issue has affected your sense of self. In any case, you see the need to take your life back.

   If you're in a significant relationship with someone who is actively addicted or otherwise needy, you might be tempted to focus on his or her issues instead of your own. To what degree do you recognize an inclination toward secondary dependency? How is it expressed?

5. What efforts have you made in the past to take your life back? How do you feel when you consider the possibility of living in freedom? Do you believe it's possible? Why or why not?

6. In order to take your life back, you're invited to face the destructive behaviors that are holding you captive. These behaviors—lying, secrecy, self-sabotage, disordered eating, self-injury, substance abuse, addictive pursuits, and other traps—harm both you and your relationships.

What destructive behaviors are you able to identify in your life?

Where have these choices taken you?

Closing Prayer

Father, thank you for this opportunity to see your face and hear your voice. Confident in you and your power, we reject the lie that transformation is not possible. We offer our lives to you with the confidence that you are leading and equipping us as we purpose to take our lives back. We give you thanks in the strong name of Jesus. Amen.

Questions for Personal Reflection

These questions are for you to consider on your own. Invite God to be your guide, and take all the time you need to notice what's inside of you.

1. Steve and David identify five primary ways in which many of us have been wounded. Which of these do you most closely identify with from your experience?

    ☐ *Mental abuse:* Someone invalidated your individuality and stifled your inner life of feelings.

    ☐ *Emotional abuse:* Someone exposed you to a behavior that resulted in psychological trauma.

    ☐ *Physical abuse:* Someone caused injury or trauma through bodily contact.

    ☐ *Sexual abuse:* Someone forced undesired sexual contact on you.

    ☐ *Spiritual abuse:* Someone distorted and misused God's Word and God's name to manipulate or control you.

Using the space below, record three or four concrete incidents for any of the previously mentioned woundings you endured.

2. Consider your parents or caregivers. Because it's natural for children to idealize their parents, many people assume that they deserve whatever they've received. We also tend to believe that what our parents said about us is entirely true. We've swallowed it whole. But now, as adults, we're able to assess whether what we received—attention, words, touch—were what we most needed.

   Let's look at what you received from your parents. The more specific you can be, the more useful this exercise will be to you.

Ways in which my father was able to accept me fully by being present physically and emotionally	Ways in which my father was unable to accept me fully by being present physically and emotionally

Ways in which my mother was able to accept me fully by being present physically and emotionally	Ways in which my mother was unable to accept me fully by being present physically and emotionally

As you recognize the gifts you've received from your parents, give thanks to God. And as you recognize the deficits from your early experience, surrender these to God.

3. "The starting point for understanding our woundedness is to recognize that our parents—and their parents before them—were also wounded people to some degree." We all were wounded to some extent as children, some more deeply than others. To name this truth is not to get stuck in blame; it is to acknowledge that perfect parents do not exist.

   From what you know of your family's history, in what ways were your father and your mother wounded?

How was their wounding passed on to you?

4. To glimpse what it means to live from your true self, take a peek at Adam and Eve in the Garden before the first cover-up.

When we operate from our *authentic* or *true* self, there is no hiding or defensive posturing. Our true self is characterized by love, caring, vulnerability, and the capacity to form deep connections with others and with God. We're in touch with our feelings, and we accept ourselves as we are. We're free to play, be spontaneous, and care for others. Living authentically from our real self is a healthy way to live. Our real self is the self that God sees.

Using the following grid, consider the relationships you have with others—at home, at work, at church, in the community, online, and in your earlier years. Notice where you've been able to be the person God created you to be, and where you've covered up, worn masks, or sought to appear as other than you really are.

For example . . .

RELATIONSHIP	Real Self	False Self
At church	*Can keep it real with my small group*	*Told people that things were great, but I've been depressed for weeks*
Social media	*Messaged Susan at a low point in my day*	*Have never once posted an unflattering picture of myself*

Where can you show your real self? Where do you cover up?

RELATIONSHIP	Real Self	False Self
At work		
At church		
In community		
With partner		
With kids		
With parents		
With extended family		
On social media		

If you need more space, continue this exercise in your personal journal.

Meditate

When you close your eyes, are you able to envision the Father's warm, kind, gracious countenance? Reread Luke 15:11-32 and take time to meditate on God's love for you. Picture yourself in relation to the father that Jesus describes. Use the list below to guide you and help you focus on what is real and true.

> » God's grace is sufficient.
> » God's mercy washes over you.
> » There is no shame.
> » There is no judgment.
> » There is no condemnation.
> » There is no recrimination.
> » There is no rejection.
> » There is only celebration.
> » God is moving toward you.
> » God is calling you to return home.
> » God is enfolding you with loving arms.

Focus on Scripture

Jesus told a story of a child returning to a father who is good:

> He returned home to his father. And while he was still
> a long way off, his father saw him coming. Filled with
> love and compassion, he ran to his son, embraced him,
> and kissed him.
>
> LUKE 15:20

This week, as you consider the story of the father who embraces the wayward child who has come home, allow yourself to receive the love the Father has for you.

> *I am returning home to my Father. As I am on my way, my Father sees me coming. Filled with love and compassion, my Father runs toward me, embraces me, and kisses me.*

Hold this story in your heart this week as a picture of what is true about your journey with the Father right now.

Take Your Life Back Experiment

Steve and David say that something special happens when we are courageous enough to share our pain and our destructive behaviors, and make ourselves accountable to someone in order to break free from those patterns.

Over the course of this five-week study, look for an opportunity to share your story with a trusted listener. This might be a friend, a relative, or a professional such as a counselor or a pastor with whom you can open up. Share with this safe person the story of where you've been and where you are headed.

Maybe you immediately thought of someone who could receive your story. Or maybe you'll pray about it this week and keep your eyes open for the person that God will provide. If it's difficult for you to identify a safe person, we will offer some help in session 4. But know that you don't have to travel on this journey alone.

When you meet with your safe and trusted person, use the following outline to guide your time together:

1. *Share your pain.* As you share your story with your trusted listener, let him or her know some of the tender spots from your journey.
2. *Share your response to your pain.* Are there destructive behaviors you've developed in response to your pain? Share these with your trusted listener.
3. *Pray.* Having done the brave work of sharing your story, commit it to God together in prayer.

Insights

Use this space to jot down any insights that arise during the group discussion or your time of personal reflection.

SESSION 2:

ROOTS OF
REACTIVE LIVING

Date of group meeting:

_____

BEFORE YOUR GROUP MEETING: Read chapters 4–6 in *Take Your Life Back*.

Introduction

Even in the best of families, the attachment between parent and child can be fraught with anxiety, fear, and uncertainty. And though in our earliest years we developed our reactions as a means of staying alive, today those same reactions keep us from living in freedom. In this session, you will have the opportunity to consider the ways in which you have reacted to the pain from your past.

To assess your readiness for this session, ask yourself the same question that Jesus asks in John 5 of the man by the pool of Bethesda who has been sick for thirty-eight years: "Would you like to get well?"

If the answer is *yes*, then you've probably already sensed a need to release your old habits and surrender to a different way of living.

As you consider the behaviors and patterns that characterize *reactive* living, you will begin to move forward with renewed purpose. You may summon the courage to take an inventory of the defects you see in your life and review them with someone who can help you see clearly. You might choose to enlist a sponsor in a Life Recovery group. You may decide to work with a counselor. As you put to the test your desire to get well, you will begin to gain traction in taking your life back.

Group Discussion

Opening Prayer
Gracious God, give us the courage to look at the roots of reactive living in our earliest years. Grant us your wisdom so that we won't become entangled in blame and shame, but will instead recognize those areas where you're inviting us to grow healthier. Yes, we would like to get well! Guide us by your Holy Spirit. Amen.

Scripture Focus

Read the story in John 5:1-15 of the man at the pool of Bethesda whom Jesus heals.

Conversation Starter

Why do you think Jesus asked a man who had been sick for almost four decades whether he wanted to get well?

As you think about your journey to take your life back, how have you failed to seize past opportunities to be made well?

What is unique about *now*—both internally and externally— that makes this moment ripe for growth and healing?

Discussion

1. Although each person is unique, in one way or another we've allowed parts of our lives to be controlled by other people, destructive patterns, or unrealistic expectations. Below are some key signals that indicate we need to *act* to take our lives back. Place a checkmark in the box next to those you recognize in your own experience.

   ☐ **We deny:** We refuse to deal with our issues, downplaying our need for change in comparison to someone else's problems. Or we deny that there's anything we can do about it.

   ☐ **We minimize:** We don't acknowledge the full scope and intensity of our struggles.

☐ **We comply:** We fall in line and absorb whatever comes our way.

☐ **We adhere:** We latch on to anyone who will have us, no matter how we're treated.

☐ **We deceive:** We refuse to see what is real and true about our lives, misleading others and ourselves.

☐ **We placate:** We give away little pieces of ourselves to appease others and reduce tension.

☐ **We cover:** We disguise, conceal, and bury the pain of our wounds with superficial treatment.

☐ **We enable:** We go along with whatever happens because we have rationalized the behavior of others. We make excuses, look the other way, or even join in to avoid conflict.

☐ **We control:** We take charge to avoid feeling powerless or hopeless—sometimes to the point of developing our own addictions, compulsions, or dependencies.

☐ **We attack:** We criticize everything that doesn't please us perfectly, destroying the people we hold responsible for our pain with our words and our disappointment.

☐ **We isolate:** We pull away from meaningful engagement and stop letting others into our lives—even those who care for us and could help us.

Share with the group an example of how one of these reactions is controlling your life right now. Also, share what will be different as you choose to release this reaction and respond from a healthier place.

2. To help us better understand what it looks like for adults to behave reactively, we can observe the behaviors of children who suffer from reactive attachment disorder (RAD). Though the condition is rare, it sheds light on the darkness of adult reactive living.

For example, when a woman we know reviewed the symptoms of RAD, the first characteristic—emotionally withdrawn behavior toward caregivers—triggered some memories from her childhood, which she otherwise would have described as *happy*. She recalled some mental snapshots of herself as a young child playing with her toys in a tiny closet, crawling under her bed to hide, and building forts out of boxes under a staircase and in a crawl space. By comparing her memories with the symptoms experienced by children with RAD, she finally was able to recognize how she had withdrawn from her caregivers to protect herself.

Though most likely you would not be diagnosed with RAD, review the symptoms below and check the box next to any that characterize your own experience. Share with the group specific ways you recognize these patterns in your adult living.

☐ *Emotionally withdrawn behavior toward caregivers*
Feeling anxiety in proximity to others, we have withdrawn into ourselves and away from connection and attachment to others. Unable to glean comfort from our closest relationships, we've found comfort in something or someone else that we have latched on to for relief. Without ever meaning to hurt ourselves or others, we have broken the link between ourselves and the healthy nurturing of our souls that we so desperately need.

☐ *Persistent social and emotional problems*
Whether we fail to regulate our emotions in an adult way and *act out*, or we stop responding to others and *react in*, we sever relationship with others by our behavior. We fear we'll be abused, neglected, or ignored as we have been before.

☐ *Persistent lack of having emotional needs met by caregivers*
Though desperate to have our needs met, we appear self-sufficient. We won't reveal our need, lest we allow someone to disappoint us and let us down again.

☐ *Limited opportunity to form stable and secure attachments*

By reacting instead of responding, we destroy stability. Though resources—support groups, counselors, therapists, workshops—are often plentiful, we refuse to enlist the help that would meet our deepest needs.

3. According to psychiatrist John Bowlby, children in a healthy mother-child relationship enjoy secure attachments. The nurturing, mothering person is a safe and stable base from which the children can venture out to explore the world before they return to the security of the mother. A stable mother is *available, responsive,* and *accepting.*

In the following diagram, if you imagine a mother sitting on a park bench as a stable base of security, the dotted lines trace the freedom of a child who is securely attached: He or she leaves the mother to explore, returns to recharge, and then goes off to explore again.

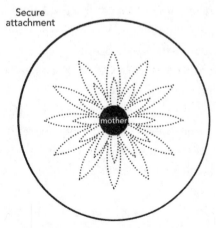

Secure
attachment

mother

Does the model of an available, responsive, accepting mother sound like what you experienced as a child? If not, what was missing from the three key components of a stable and secure mother-child relationship? How might your mother have behaved differently to provide what you needed the most?

Was there someone in your life—teacher, aunt, grandparent, neighbor, mother of a friend—whom you perceived to be an available, responsive, accepting mother? Describe the specific encounters with her that signaled this to you.

4. Though many of us suffered broken attachments in childhood, we were not designed to live reactive lives. God wired us to connect with other people. Stephen Arterburn and David Stoop believe that we can not only survive broken attachments, but even thrive.

   When children experience insecure attachments, the mother isn't perceived as a source of safety and security. The following diagram shows avoidant, ambivalent, anxious, and fearful attachments to a mother who's not a stable, secure base of support.

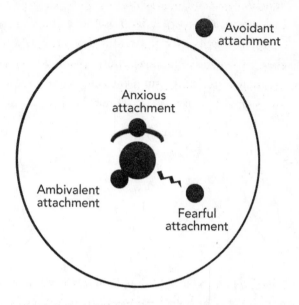

In *avoidant* attachments, the mother is preoccupied with herself and offers little attentiveness to the child. The child mirrors the mother's indifference, and both mother and child demonstrate indifference toward the other.

When a child experiences an *ambivalent* attachment, he or she clings to the mother, who is anxious about letting the child explore. The child absorbs the mother's anxiety and reflects her ambivalence.

When parent and child roles are reversed and a child must become the "responsible parent" to an incompetent adult, the child experiences an *anxious* attachment.

Children who have endured abuse experience *fearful*

attachments. They don't know whether they'll be embraced by loving arms or struck by those same arms.

Identify which of these four attachments aligns most closely with your experience, and explain why.

Share with the group a memory from your childhood that signals one of these attachments.

5. People who need to take their lives back tend to err in one of two ways. Some believe they should never say anything bad about their parents because their parents did the best they could. People at the other end of the spectrum are prone to becoming stuck in criticism and blame.

Only positive . . . Able to recognize positive and negative . . . Only negative

$$\longleftarrow \hspace{6cm} \longrightarrow$$

Share where you find yourself on this continuum and explain why.

If you have siblings, where would you place them on this scale? If their memories and experience were different from yours, why do you imagine that might be?

We take back our lives as we remember and understand what happened during childhood, place and accept responsibility where it belongs, grieve what was lost, protect ourselves from repetitive hurtful behaviors, and, ultimately, forgive our parents.

Today, what needs to happen for you to move toward health as you take your life back?

Closing Prayer
Jesus, as a good physician, you are healing our wounded places. Thank you for being even more committed to our recovery than we are. When this process makes us uncomfortable, gird us with courage and fill us with hope so that we may glorify you by living from our real self. We continue to surrender ourselves to your Holy Spirit, who guides us on this journey, with the confidence that our lives belong to you. Amen.

Questions for Personal Reflection

1. Each person who lives reactively employs a unique combination of defenses to avoid facing what was and what is. As you're able to identify which defenses you've hidden behind, visualize what will be different as you become healthy.

    - denying
    - minimizing
    - complying
    - adhering
    - deceiving
    - placating
    - covering
    - enabling
    - controlling
    - attacking
    - isolating

    (For a discussion of these eleven common reactions to pain, see chapter 4 in *Take Your Life Back*.)

    Complete the following sentence with the reactive pattern(s) that have kept you stuck, and begin to imagine what can change when you take your life back:

    When I stop _____, *then*_____

    _____.

For example:

When I stop <u>minimizing</u>, then <u>I'll lose my excuse to do nothing to change my life</u>.

When I stop <u>isolating</u>, then <u>I'll have access to a community of support</u>.

When I stop _____, *then* _____
_____.

When I stop _____, *then* _____
_____.

When I stop _____, *then* _____
_____.

How do you feel when you think about the possibility of living differently? Describe how you imagine your relationships could change when you take your life back.

2. A 1987 study by psychologists Cindy Hazan and Phillip Shaver, based on attachment research by John Bowlby, revealed correlations between adult romantic relationships and the ways that babies respond to their caregivers.[1] Because most people's earliest memories begin after the age of two, you may need to use other clues as you consider your early attachments—perhaps memories of later experiences with your caregiver(s), family stories, or photographs. From all you know about your earliest caregivers, make an informed guess about your earliest experiences.

	Secure Attachment	Insecure Attachment
Infancy	☐ I felt safe in the arms of my caregiver(s). ☐ I enjoyed close, intimate, bodily contact with a caregiver. ☐ I felt naturally anxious when my caregiver was out of sight. ☐ I enjoyed sharing new discoveries with my caregiver(s). ☐ A caregiver and I were mutually fascinated and preoccupied with one another. ☐ My caregiver engaged in baby talk with me.	☐ I didn't feel safe and secure in the presence of a caregiver who responded to my needs. ☐ I felt isolated and alone. ☐ I felt terror when my caregiver was unresponsive to my needs. ☐ My caregiver wasn't alert to my new discoveries about myself and the world. ☐ My caregiver wasn't tuned in to me. ☐ My caregiver was aloof and detached.

	Secure Attachment	Insecure Attachment
Adulthood	☐ I feel safe in the arms of my spouse. ☐ I enjoy close, intimate bodily contact with my spouse. ☐ I find it unpleasant when my loved one is not accessible. ☐ I enjoy sharing new discoveries—about myself and my world—with my spouse. ☐ My spouse and I enjoy a fascination and mutual preoccupation with one another. ☐ My spouse and I engage in baby talk and shared humor, winks and nods.	☐ I've sought the familiarity of an uncomfortable relationship by attaching to anyone who would have me. ☐ I pursued sexual involvement before marriage in search of attachment. ☐ I feel afraid that my loved one will not return or I feel relief when he or she is away. ☐ I tend to protect, hide, cover up, and become secretive. ☐ My spouse and I are frustrated with one another, evaluating and second-guessing everything we do or intend to do. ☐ One of us takes on the role of a shaming, displeased parent while the other becomes like a child or servant.

Would you describe your relationship with your earliest caregiver(s) as *secure* or *insecure*?

Describe a specific example from your experience that best reflects your answer.

How do you believe this early attachment experience affected your subsequent relationships?

The connections between our earliest relationships and our adult ones are often uncanny. Share your thoughts on those connections in your own relationships, both romantic and platonic.

3. One of the ways in which we live reactively in relation to early insecure attachments is by attaching to something or someone in order to find comfort or relief. We might attach to a person; to an obsession or compulsion; or to food, drink, or drugs—anything that promises to soothe our hurting hearts. Because we have needed to believe that we were okay, we may have denied that our substitute attachment was unhealthy.

Asking God to guide your heart and mind, list any substitutes you may have attached yourself to over the years.

Which ones have you since found freedom from? What precipitated that freedom? Which ones do you still cling to?

Meditate

Imagine Jesus sitting by your side. Close your eyes, take a deep breath, and mentally revisit your childhood. Starting with your infancy, glance briefly over each year and decade of your life from birth until now, holding in your heart the reality that Jesus has been present in every moment of your life. Commit these memories to God.

Hear Jesus ask you, "Would you like to get well?"

How do you respond?

If you answer *no*, Jesus will honor your wish. He will not force you.

If you answer *yes*, Jesus may invite you to look more closely at some of the moments on that timeline of your life.

Take all the time you need with Jesus, observing and reflecting on your journey. Record significant details and insights in your journal.

Focus on Scripture

Remember the man whom Jesus healed at the pool of Bethesda?

After healing the man, Jesus disappeared into the crowd before the man could ask his name. Later, though, Jesus found the man in the Temple, and that's when the man realized that it was Jesus who had healed him.

It's time for you to realize that Jesus is healing *you*. As you venture into the new life that God has for you—even if your steps are tentative and shaky—you are progressively being healed. In the name of Jesus, God will provide the resources you need in order to grow, and the Holy Spirit will strengthen you to do the work that lies before you.

This week, cling to these words: *Jesus is healing me.*

Take Your Life Back Experiment

This may be the first time you've considered the quality of your attachments to your earliest caregivers.

If you have access to old family photos, pull them out. As you browse through pictures of yourself at different ages—early infancy, toddlerhood, childhood—consider the nature of your attachments to your primary caregivers. Though you're considering *emotional* attachment, photos showing physical proximity may give clues to, or elicit feelings about, how safe and secure you felt in the presence of the important adults in your life.

What can you glean or remember about your relationship with your mother? What about with your father?

If you don't have access to childhood photos, get some paper and draw a few of your earliest memories with caregivers. (If art is not your thing, you can jot down a few words that encapsulate your memories.) What can you glean from these memories about your earliest attachments?

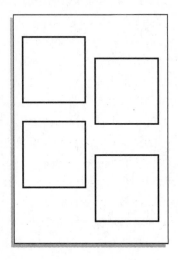

Insights

Use this space to jot down any insights that arise during the group discussion or your time of personal reflection.

SESSION 3:

SHAME, TRAUMA, AND LOSING YOURSELF

Date of group meeting:

BEFORE YOUR GROUP MEETING: Read chapters 7–10 in *Take Your Life Back*.

Introduction

This is the last session we'll spend looking at the reactive life before we move on to discover and embrace a new way of living.

Though it may be tempting to try to skim through the hard work that needs to be done—because maybe it feels safer?—you will gain the most from these exercises if you're able to give yourself fully to the process.

As you become more willing to recognize the ways in which your reactions to toxic shame and trauma have caused you to lose your real self and lose touch with your soul, you will become equipped to take your life back.

We lose our real self when we don't believe that others will accept who we really are. We put on masks to hide our shame and show a better face to the world. But if we are to be released from shame so that we can rediscover our true self—the beloved self that God sees—we must press on to accomplish the bold work of facing what is really inside of us. As we gather our courage to look at what we have endured and how it has shaped us, we move ever closer to health and well-being.

In everything, we can be assured that God is with us, guiding and comforting us, as we face the truth of our inner world.

Group Discussion

Opening Prayer

God of grace, you are the one in whom we find our lives. Thank you for knitting us together and calling us your own. Continue to be our faithful guide as we face what we've avoided and seek to take our lives back. We pray this for the sake of your Kingdom and our souls. Amen.

Scripture Focus

Read Luke 18:10-14, the story of the two men who went to the Temple to pray.

Conversation Starter

As you consider Luke's account of the story Jesus told about two men who went to pray in the Temple, review what you have learned about the true self and the false self.

In what ways might the Pharisee be operating from a false self?

In what ways does the tax collector model what it means to connect with our real self?

Putting yourself in the shoes of the two men, why do you suppose the Pharisee—or a modern-day churchgoer—would feel the need to present a false self to others? And why would the tax collector finally get honest about who he really is?

Which one do you most relate to today? Why?

Discussion

1. Stephen Arterburn and David Stoop explain the difference between *toxic shame* and *good shame*. Toxic shame convinces us that we're worthless, bad, and hopelessly stuck. It wrongly fuses our *experience* (of abandonment, mistreatment, or abuse) and our *behavior* (the poor choices we make) with our *identity*.

    Good shame—which the authors equate with *godly sorrow*—distinguishes our identity from what we've endured and even some of what we've chosen. In this way, good shame draws our attention to the areas of our lives where we need to make some adjustments.

As you read the statements below, choose between those that signal *toxic shame* and those that indicate *good shame*.[2]

T	G	I am worthless garbage to be discarded.
T	G	I shouldn't have left my wife and kids.
T	G	I'm not worth loving.
T	G	I feel guilty for hitting my wife.
T	G	I'm not worth showing up for.
T	G	I shouldn't be cheating on my husband.
T	G	I'm not worth protecting.
T	G	I feel awful for lying to my parents.
T	G	I'm not worth sticking around for.
T	G	I'm mortified that I got drunk last night.

Discuss your answers as a group.

In your own words, how would you describe to a friend the difference between toxic shame and good shame?

2. In response to the trauma we have endured, or in reaction to an unhealthy person, we may have learned that it was safer to repress our feelings than to acknowledge them. Yet,

in burying our negative emotions, we have inadvertently buried other emotions as well.

At times, we have *underreacted*, unable to feel sorrow when grieving a loss. At other times, we have *overreacted*, blowing up at something insignificant with an incongruent emotion, when sadness or fear might have been the real emotion we were having difficulty accessing.

Describe a situation in which you've had trouble expressing healthy emotions. Specifically, how did your underreaction or overreaction affect your relationships? Which emotion—e.g., anger, sadness, fear, joy—was appropriate to the situation, and which emotion did you express?

3. The false self we show to others communicates that we're something other than what we actually are. As you consider the various arenas of your life—work, school, church, community, family—name some occasions when you have presented a false self to others in order to appear more poised, attractive, intelligent, spiritual, clever, social, athletic, etc.

Does the mask of a false self allow you to connect more deeply with others, or does it distance you? Describe an encounter when you could see the difference.

4. Steve and David tell the stories of Bob (who performed to secure his parents' good favor) and Mary (who imitated her mother by choosing and enabling an alcoholic spouse), who both lost touch with their souls when they were young. They both developed lives that revolved around taking care of or meeting the expectations of someone else.

Until we do the work to unbury our real self, we'll stay stuck in all our relationships. Our goal in taking our lives back is to realign with our true self so we can develop healthy, loving, and open relationships in which we feel accepted and affirmed for who we are rather than for what we do.

Look back on your early life, and even your recent past, and share an instance or two of a time when you were living for someone else. What did that look like? What was lost because of it?

5. Though we're all tempted to put on masks and show a false self to the world, there are some people who have refused to live from a false self. Do you know someone like this? Examples would include the following:

- a woman who accepts her appearance and doesn't try to look like someone else
- a man who doesn't try to hide his addiction or his recovery journey
- a teenager who refuses to squeeze into someone else's mold
- an older adult who is more interested in investing in others than in grasping after life's pleasures

People who live from an authentic self are in touch with their feelings and accept themselves as they are. People who live authentically are able to be vulnerable and form deep connections with others and with God. Simply put, people who live from their real self are the same person in every situation.

Share with the group about a person you know who lives most consistently from his or her authentic self. How is this expressed in the individual's relationships with others?

Closing Prayer

God, you know us better than we know ourselves. Though we once cared most about the opinions of others, we are now deciding to be transparent before you and authentic with others. This week, give us the courage to be real in our relationships. Shine your light into the darkest recesses of our hearts and expose what we've tried to bury and conceal. Amen.

Questions for Personal Reflection

1. Trauma occurs when a stressful event destroys our sense of security and leaves us vulnerable or in a state of helplessness. There is no "standard" for traumatic events by which to gauge the impact on an individual. For example, a terrified toddler quarantined in a hospital for two weeks may experience more enduring traumatic effects than a resilient child who spends two years in an orphanage.

   In your earliest years, can you identify a trauma—either one recognized by those around you or one known only to you—that has affected your sense of self or well-being? How has this trauma affected your adult relationships?

2. If we were hurt or traumatized as children by someone we depended on, perhaps we didn't feel it was safe for us to hold our caregivers responsible, so we blamed ourselves. Specifically, the voice of shame capitalized on what we endured—abuse, neglect, abandonment, mistreatment— and convinced us that we deserved what we got.

   As we are able to connect our experience—that which we did not deserve—with the messages we internalized and believed about that experience, we can begin to move toward freedom.

   For example, a child who was relinquished for adoption or whose parents divorced may believe that he or she "wasn't worth sticking around for" or "wasn't worth loving." Though an outside observer might reason otherwise, an adult with this history may still be controlled by toxic shame.

   In the following chart, make note of the experiences that distorted or damaged your real self, noting what shaming messages you may have believed about your experience.

What I Endured	What I Believed (Toxic Shame)
Parents divorced	"I'm not worth sticking around for."

When you're able to recognize the shaming messages you've internalized, you can replace them with affirmations of truth. If you have trouble with this, invite a friend who is also on a healing journey, possibly someone in your group, to help you. You can offer each other a fresh set of eyes and ears.

What I Endured	What Is True (Statements of Affirmation)
Parents divorced	"I am God's beloved child. I am worth loving."

If you need more space, use your personal journal to explore the messages you internalized.

3. Every day, we are tempted to present a false self to appear more poised, attractive, intelligent, spiritual, clever, social, athletic, etc. In your group meeting, were you able to share an example of a time when you put on a mask to appear

better than you are? If not, what kept you from allowing others to see who you really are?

Take some quiet time to consider what might happen if you refused to show others a false self.

- What's the worst that could happen if you showed others who you really are?

- What's the best thing that could happen if you showed others who you really are?

- Are you willing to experiment with lowering your mask? Why or why not?

4. Many of us struggle in our relationship with God because we've buried our real self. Trying to play it safe, fearing that our real self is too damaged, we don't want to be truly known, not even by God. But our desire to be fully received and embraced for who we are will never be met if we continue to bury our real self and offer only a weak façade in its place.

   If you were to humbly choose life by showing God the very ugliest parts of yourself that you'd prefer to remain hidden, what would you reveal?

Have you ever been able to reveal these parts of yourself to a safe person in your life? Why or why not?

Meditate

Spend some time reflecting on the transforming truth that God is delighted in you. He welcomes every beautiful and broken part of your real self that you are willing to offer.

Practice silent reverence, allowing everything within you to worship and honor God.

After a time of silence—you may want to set an alarm for ten or fifteen minutes so you don't worry about the time—receive Jesus' gracious, life-giving word to you: "I tell you, this sinner, not the Pharisee, returned home justified before God" (Luke 18:14).

Focus on Scripture

Consider the two men who went to the Temple to pray (Luke 18:10-14). Specifically, recall the Pharisee, who separated himself by announcing, "I thank you, God, that I am not like other people—cheaters, sinners, adulterers. I'm certainly not like that tax collector! I fast twice a week, and I give you a tenth of my income" (Luke 18:11-12).

There's a little bit of Pharisee in all of us, so get real with God this week by turning the Pharisee's words upside down and inside out:

> I confess, God, that I am very much like other
> people—cheaters, sinners, adulterers. I'm even like the
> sinner next to me from whom I've tried to separate
> myself. I fail to honor you with my body and with my
> money.

Who is the "sinner" in your life to whom you favorably compare yourself? The person you don't want to be like? It may be relative or someone else you're close to.

Make the tax collector's prayer and the upside-down prayer of the Pharisee your prayers this week.

Take Your Life Back Experiment

Toxic shame festers and grows when it lives in the dark. But as you're able to expose it to light—replacing lies with truth—shame's grip is weakened.

During your personal reflection this week, you identified some of the beliefs you've held that resulted from earlier trauma. You also had the opportunity to replace those beliefs with truth that aligns with what God says about your real self.

Choose one of those new beliefs about God or yourself—"God can be trusted," "I'm worth loving," "I am God's beloved child"—and make it a phrase that you repeat to yourself throughout the week.

Make it visible: Post it on social media, tape it to your dashboard, write it on your lunch bag.

Insights

Use this space to jot down any insights that arise during the group discussion or your time of personal reflection.

TAKING YOUR LIFE BACK

Date of group meeting:

BEFORE YOUR GROUP MEETING: Read the Reintroduction to part II as well as chapters 11–12 in *Take Your Life Back*.

Introduction

Now that you've done the hard work of looking at your early life to understand the ways you were living reactively, we're going to explore the better alternative: *responsive living*. This is a healthy way of living that you can begin to choose today.

To get the big-picture view of this life-giving way, consider three distinct shifts you will notice as you decide to live responsively.

» You will begin to see, and believe, that you have choices you can make.
» You will develop a trusting relationship with another person. You will also learn to trust God and trust yourself.
» You will learn to identify your feelings.

The choice to live responsively isn't like jumping off a cliff. It's more like walking along a pathway. It takes some effort, but you will eventually arrive at your destination. Of course, there will be bumps along the way. You may experience painful feelings. You may find yourself returning to old patterns of behavior. But as you reflect on those situations, you'll learn to identify which emotions you were feeling at the time. Eventually, you will be able to get in touch with your emotions in real time, as you're experiencing them.

Group Discussion

Opening Prayer
Father, thank you for inviting us into a life of hope and promise. As we step into a new way of living, give us the courage to feel and the confidence that you will never leave us or forsake us. We thank you that our lives can be different than they've been, and we trust you to lead us. Amen.

Scripture Focus

Don't copy the behavior and customs of this world,
but let God transform you into a new person by
changing the way you think. Then you will learn to
know God's will for you, which is good and pleasing
and perfect.

ROMANS 12:2

Conversation Starter

Because Paul exhorts us not to copy the behavior and customs
of this world, it seems he knows how we operate. He also knows
that the way to *change* is by allowing God to transform the way
we *think*.

Are there ways in which you've copied the unhealthy behaviors of the formative adults in your life? Maybe you vowed that
you'd be nothing like those who raised you. Unfortunately, that
means they're still in control.

Maybe you disconnect in a passive-aggressive way like your
mother did; or maybe you explode in anger like your dad.
Maybe you've mirrored the addiction that once wounded you
and is now wounding others.

Share with the group how you've reacted—by either imitating or living in opposition to the behaviors of those around
you.

Imagine how your life would be different today—how it
can be different—if you chose to live *responsively* rather than
reactively. Share your insights with the group.

Discussion

As you begin to implement the new skills you're learning, it may be helpful to think about and identify how you were living until now, and how your life will look different today and in the future.

1. Describe an incident from your adult life when you *reacted* because you believed you had no choice. What was the situation, who was involved, and how did the incident unfold?

Now that you know that you have choices, share at least two different ways you might have responded to the same situation. If you get stuck, invite the group to suggest possibilities.

2. Share with the group a moment from your childhood that convinced you that others were not to be trusted. Who was involved, and what happened?

Describe a time from your adult life when you lived *reactively* because you weren't able to trust someone. (This may have been expressed as an unhealthy dependence or unhealthy independence.)

3. Name one person in your life today whom you deem to be worthy of your trust. What is it about this person that makes trust possible?

How is your relationship with this person different from the relationship early in your life that wounded you?

4. When you were young, you learned to read the emotions of others in order to survive, and you buried your own feelings, making them difficult to access.

Today, you can choose to notice and identify what you're feeling in any situation. (It takes practice, but you'll get there.) As you give your "frozen feelings" permission to thaw, they will.

As you think of your experience over the past seven days or so, identify a situation in which you felt

- Joy
- Sadness
- Fear
- Anger

Share one recent feeling with the group, as well as the situation that precipitated it.

If noticing your feelings is a new experience, consider recording them in a journal. Developing the habit will prime you to notice your feelings and begin to understand the signals they're sending you.

5. It's helpful to identify your basic emotional posture when faced with high stress or an emotional crisis. Which of the following four emotions—fear, anger, toxic shame, sadness—feel the most familiar to you today?

FEAR

Almost every codependent behavior pattern begins with a posture of fear. If you are operating out of fear, you might hold questions like these in your heart:

- Will they like me?
- Will they accept me?
- Will they be nice to me?

ANGER

If you're overly focused on other people's problems, or if you still need to process some deep hurts, you may find that you approach relationships from a posture of anger. If you are operating out of anger, you might hold questions like these in your heart:

- Why is it always up to me?
- Why can't they handle this better?

TOXIC SHAME

If you've become stuck viewing yourself according to the way you were treated when you were growing up, you may be in a posture of toxic shame. If you are operating out of toxic shame, you might hold questions like these in your heart:

- What's wrong with me?
- Why am I not good enough?

SADNESS

If you're stuck in grief, bound by overwhelming feelings of loss, you may be in a posture of sadness. If you are operating out of sadness, you might hold questions like these in your heart:

- Why do I hurt so much?
- Will this ever end?

Share with the group a concrete example of a highly stressful situation in which you noticed that you had assumed a posture of fear, anger, shame, or sadness. What triggered that reaction?

If you found yourself in that same situation tomorrow, what truth—about who you are or who God is—would help you avoid reverting to a posture of fear, anger, shame, or sadness?

Closing Prayer

God, we've admitted that we are powerless over our problems, and we've put our hope for redemption in you. This week we offer our lives to you with the confidence that you are the author of transformation. Quicken our minds to recognize the thoughts that have kept us bound up, and change the way we think so that we may flourish and bring you glory. Amen.

Questions for Personal Reflection

1. In your first group session, you were invited to identify and speak to a safe person. In chapter 11 of *Take Your Life Back*, Steve and David unpack the idea a bit further, suggesting that you find a safe person with whom to share the healing journey. This person might be someone with whom you have a personal relationship, or it might be a professional counselor. Here are some traits that characterize a safe person:

   ☑ A safe person listens to understand.
   ☑ A safe person doesn't make everything about himself or herself.
   ☑ A safe person keeps a confidence.
   ☑ A safe person is someone you can trust.

Make a list of people you know who would qualify as safe for you. Prayerfully offer your list to God and ask for his help in discerning whom you should approach.

2. One of the most powerful actions you can take is to give a name to what happened to you. It is about speaking the truth. To name something is to take authority over it. It is an empowering action.

Name what happened to you by filling in the blanks:

> *I'm a recovering codependent who* _____
> _____. *I'm going to name*
> *that period in my life* _____,
> *and I am now in* _____
> _____.

You might say something like this: "I'm a recovering codependent who was <u>physically abused as a child</u>. I'm going to name that period in my life <u>'my time of instability,'</u> and I am now in <u>'the solid place.'</u>"

Here are three important components of naming what is true:

- Name what you endured.
- Identify what you endured as a season in the past. (Make it about you and not someone else.)
- Identify your current season as one of life and health.

Describe how your bold announcement makes you feel.

Consider writing your "naming statement" on a card and taping it to your bathroom mirror (or inside your Bible for more privacy).

3. As you acknowledge the truth about what has happened to you, it becomes very clear that something was lost during that time and is still lost today. Based on what you have learned about your woundedness, abandonment issues, fears, anger, and shame, you can say that the primary loss has been the loss of your real self.

    By identifying the losses you are going to grieve, you will begin to grapple with two interwoven facets of grief: *anger* and *sadness*. Steve and David suggest that men tend to embrace the anger (protest) part of grieving and women are more likely to embrace the sadness (resignation).

    How would you say that these generalized gender patterns are true or untrue for you?

Consider your own expression of grief. Color in the following pie chart to show how much of your grief has been expressed as *sadness*. Outline the sections showing how much of your grief has been expressed as *anger*.

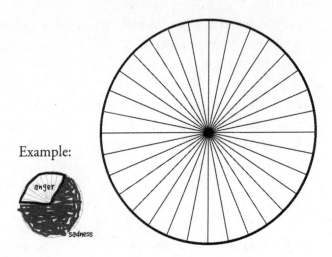

Example:

Which part of your pie is smaller? You may find it useful to explore this smaller portion.

Notice which expression is more difficult for you and write either a sad letter or an angry letter to those who withheld from you what you needed or were responsible for what you lost. This letter is for your eyes only. You may choose to share it with your safe person, but it should go no further. It's a tool to help you grieve.

4. It's often easier to identify someone else's problems and remain blind to our own. It makes sense: Noticing our own shortcomings is uncomfortable because it can evoke feelings of shame, guilt, or fear. When our eyes are opened to our own fallibility, we become responsible for changing.

We hope you hear the good news in that statement: You can *choose* to change. In fact, changing your thinking is transformational because it takes your focus away from everything in front of you and places it firmly on everything *within* you.

If we're to make the shift from wasting energy on what we have no ability to change to pouring it into what we are able to change, we need to recognize where we've been squandering our energy.

List the names (or, for confidentiality, use initials or a secret code name that only you would know) of two or three people who are close to you and whose faults and foibles you are intimately acquainted with. (No need to chronicle the faults.)

Now shift your attention back to yourself.

Remember, you have the ability to *decide* to trust God, yourself, and others and to acknowledge your feelings. Given this ability, what can you decide to do differently in order to release each individual you've named above, and take your life back?

Here's a rule of thumb for when you're feeling stuck:

Don't think: *I can change the other person.*

Decide to start thinking: *I can change myself, no matter what the other person does.*

List the choices you can make for yourself, no matter what the other person does:

5. In the process of taking your life back, grief must lead to forgiveness. Having experienced radical undeserved forgiveness from God, there is nothing we've endured that is beyond forgiveness. It may take time, but it is both possible and liberating.

   Forgiveness isn't a feeling, it's a decision. Make a list—short or long—of the people you need to forgive. Pray through your list now, and continue to do it regularly, confirming your decision to forgive.

Meditate

Once you have realized that change is possible, you still must be *willing* to change. Are you?

Set a timer and spend fifteen minutes reflecting on your willingness to change. Ask God to illumine your heart and mind as you consider two conflicting choices:

» How am I willing to change?
» How am I unwilling to change?

Notice any resistance that surfaces. Picture how your life will be different when you're able to live the way God designed you to live.

Offer back to God both your resistance to change and your willingness to embrace the beautiful future you imagined for yourself.

Focus on Scripture

The apostle Paul challenged the Christians in Rome, "Don't copy the behavior and customs of this world, but let God transform you into a new person by changing the way you think" (Romans 12:2). Paul understood how to take your life back—with God's help!

This week, let Paul's admonition be the prayer on your lips: *God, transform me by changing the way I think.* Allow these words to open the eyes and ears of your heart.

Take Your Life Back Experiment

If you have dependency issues, you already know how to be compassionate toward other people. It's obvious how to care for others, but it's less obvious how to care for ourselves. Change isn't easy, but it's possible. Try this exercise.

1. Recall a situation from your earliest years that's still unresolved for you. Perhaps it was a pivotal experience that still haunts you, or maybe it was a seemingly insignificant incident that caused you to feel alone or misunderstood.

2. Bring to mind the details of this experience.

   - Where were you?
   - Who was there?
   - What happened?
   - How did you feel?
   - How did you respond?
   - Any other details?

3. Using your imagination, enter the scene as an adult and imagine yourself talking to the young you.

- Ask your younger self what you are feeling, and listen to the response.
- Offer your younger self the comfort you longed to receive at the time. Take all the time you need, imagining your adult self embracing your younger self, offering comfort and acceptance. If tears surface, let them flow freely.
- List some ways in which you can begin to better *defend* yourself.

4. When you have finished comforting your younger self, tuck him or her in safely and leave the scene.

5. Recap the experiment in one of two ways:

- Journal what you experienced during the experiment.
- Call your safe person and share your experience from the experiment.
- Practice taking on the role of *developer* by beginning to ask and answer the question, "*Now* what do I need to do?"

You may want to repeat this exercise at a different time, using other scenarios in which your adult self offers comfort and compassion to your younger self.

Insights

Use this space to jot down any insights that arise during the group discussion or your time of personal reflection.

SESSION 5:

HEALTH ON THE JOURNEY

Date of group meeting:

_____

BEFORE YOUR GROUP MEETING: Read chapters 13–14 in *Take Your Life Back*.

Introduction

Taking your life back involves both an external journey—noticing what's happening outside of you, in relation to others—and also an internal journey—noticing what's happening inside of you. You must be willing to do both in order to take your life back.

The external journey is about erecting and maintaining healthy boundaries. Steve and David believe that using a strong, healthy *no* can be so much more life-giving than offering an easy, passive *yes*. Establishing good boundaries changes relationships and provides hope in the most difficult circumstances. When you choose to use a good no and a good yes, you gain access to valuable tools you can use in every situation.

The internal journey involves acknowledging the truth about your past and renewing your mind by changing the way you think. As you gather resources and useful tools for the journey, you may find that working the Twelve Steps of Life Recovery with your safe person is an indispensable part of taking your life back. The Twelve Steps have proven useful and powerful for so many people, and they can be useful for you as well.

As you know by now, taking your life back isn't a five-week process. This workbook is a catalyst for a lifelong journey. You have the tools to choose to live with freedom and authenticity. Now it's up to you to use them.

Group Discussion

Opening Prayer

Father, we believe that this journey to take our lives back is part of your good plan for our lives. Thank you for being our guide and our rock as we step into the good life you have for us, and as we shed our false selves and reconnect with our real self. Give us the courage to press on, in Jesus' name. Amen.

Scripture Focus

Confess your sins to each other and pray for each
other so that you may be healed. The earnest prayer
of a righteous person has great power and produces
wonderful results.

JAMES 5:16

Conversation Starter

James's admonition to the early church suggests that recovery isn't something that happens in isolation. Rather, we experience real power and gain traction in our lives when we choose vulnerability by sharing our sins and wounds with one another.

In session 4, during your personal reflection time, you made a list of people whom you consider safe. Share with the group the qualities of a safe person that make him or her a reliable and faithful traveler on the journey toward taking your life back.

Discussion

1. Steve and David observe, "Walls of protection can definitely keep us from getting hurt, but they also will damage a relationship if they offer no way for the other person to break through. It helps to be aware of the walls we've built, and to be willing to destroy those walls and replace them with firm but flexible borders that allow others to get through and connect with us heart to heart."

   Close your eyes and imagine the "terrain" around your heart. What picture begins to emerge? An unmarked perimeter that allows anyone to come and go as they please? A firm but flexible border that lets some people in and keeps others out? A high, unscalable wall that no one can penetrate?

Share with your group the image that came to mind as you visualized the territory around your heart. (Is it a wall of eggshells? A trail of jelly beans? A moat of fiery lava? Allow your mind to be creative.)

2. Steve and David offer some helpful guidelines to help you decide when saying no makes more sense than saying yes.

WHEN TO SAY NO:

☐ Before we say *no*, we must be certain we are denying or rejecting what is wrong and defective, and not saying *no* for some other reason.

☐ Say *no* when saying *yes* would enable or encourage evil.

☐ *No* is always the right answer when our health or welfare is needlessly jeopardized by a controlling or manipulative person.

☐ Say *no* when the reason for saying *yes* would be only to avoid conflict or avoid exerting energy.

☐ Say *no* to something good when we can say *yes* to something better.

☐ Say *no* when we are tempted to repeat the same old failed strategies that have never helped us take our lives back, and never will.

WHEN *NOT* TO SAY NO:

☐ *No* is never the right answer when it's given out of fear, withholding, acting in, or revenge.

☐ We must not say *no* when we are called upon to be courageous. We must do what needs to be done, when it needs to be done, no matter the consequences.

☐ *No* is never the right answer when it is punitive, vengeful, mean, or manipulative of another person.

☐ *No* is never the right answer when *yes* would open the door of opportunity for healing and wholeness.

☐ *No* is never the right answer just because it feels safe. God would have us risk a little more to experience his fullness in our lives.

Consider one or two of the following scenarios, weighing them against the guidelines above, and discuss whether a solid *no* or a strong *yes* is in order, and why. (If it's helpful, you can add details to each to fill out a more complete picture.) How would you handle each one?

Melanie's mother has invited her over for dinner. Melanie anticipates that her mother will be drinking and knows that she can get belligerent and verbally abusive when she drinks. Should Melanie say yes or no? Why?

Sam has been sober for five months, working a Twelve-Step program and staying away from places where alcohol is served. His girlfriend has invited him to a family function where there will be alcohol, so that he can meet her parents. Should Sam say yes or no? Why?

Sandra and Paul, parents of nine-year-old twins, are legally divorced after Paul's infidelity. Sandra, who is still in pain, has previously dropped off her daughters at the home Paul shares with the woman he's involved with, but on this day Paul invites her inside. Should Sandra say yes or no? Why?

Joel was abused as a child by his domineering mother. As a result, anxiety has kept him from dating now that he's an adult. A friend from church wants to set Joel up with a woman he knows. Joel is ambivalent. Should he say yes or no? Why?

As you discuss what Melanie, Sam, Sandra, and Joel should do, be sure to support your answer with principles from the guidelines provided.

3. What about your own relationships? Implementing firm but flexible borders can be a life-changing way to take your life back. When we bravely use *no* as a positive response and offer our best *yes*, we are freed from our old patterns of dependency.

   Share with the group a recent opportunity you had to establish a healthy perimeter in your life by using a strong, brave *no*; or a recent choice to live freely by gently relaxing a wall by saying *yes*. What was the outcome?

4. *Why?* people and *why should I?* people have their default answer set to *no*. As a result, they miss chances to grow and change. But *why not?* people are open to change and opportunity. Though they're aware that a no may be in order, and they have the courage to use it, they remain open to possibility thinking.

   Which is your natural style—*why?* or *why not?*—and how is it working for you? Which is naturally easier, and which is more difficult? Share an example of a recent encounter where you chose between *why?* and *why not?*

5. Often people try to present the best version of themselves at church and are often reticent to share any of their struggles there. Unfortunately, that's not how healing works, and it's not the way the church was meant to function. God has designed something so much better for us.

What has been your experience with this kind of cover-up at church? What are some of the indicators that signal whether it's safe to lower your mask?

Share a story with the group about a time when you saw the church functioning properly as a place where it's safe for people to expose their woundedness and receive prayer for healing.

6. Life Recovery cannot be accomplished in isolation. Who have been the most valuable partners on your journey to take your life back? Share this with the group.

☐ spouse or partner
☐ friend
☐ pastor
☐ therapist
☐ another helping professional
☐ other _____

As you review this list and listen to others share, who might you seek out to strengthen your own circle of support?

7. In the back of this workbook, you will find a 31-Day Guide for Incorporating Truth into Your Daily Life. This resource will help you live out all you've learned from Stephen Arterburn and David Stoop in *Take Your Life Back*. (You can also find a printable version online at www.takeyourlifeback.tv.) As you look through these thirty-one choices, take note of which ones will give you the most traction in taking your life back.

Share with your group which of these affirmations is the one you most need to choose for today.

Based on what others in the group know about your unique story, invite individuals to suggest which of these affirmations they imagine will be the most powerful for you. Receive these affirmations as a blessing from your group.

» **Seeing:** Rejecting distortions and manipulation of the truth, I choose to see others as they really are and to see myself as I really am.
» **Surrendering:** Resisting the urge to take control, I choose to surrender to God and his wisdom.
» **Feeling:** Refusing to numb myself, I choose to honor my feelings and what I can learn from them.
» **Believing:** Rejecting crippling doubt, I choose to believe that God is real and that he cares for me.
» **Healing:** Allowing nothing or no one to take control over me, I surrender to the healing power of the Holy Spirit.
» **Choosing:** Refusing to believe the lie that I am stuck forever, I exercise my freedom to choose to *do the next right thing.*
» **Searching:** Rejecting distortion and manipulation, I search for wisdom and truth from God to guide me in all I do.
» **Connecting:** Rejecting isolation, detachment, and darkness, I choose to connect with God and others and to walk in the light.

» **Belonging:** No longer feeling rejected or abandoned, I recognize that I am included. I belong to God and to God's people.

» **Receiving:** No longer bound by the demands and neediness of others, I receive from God and from others.

» **Agreeing:** Renouncing half-truths, shame, and toxic distortions of reality, I agree with truth and everything that brings life.

» **Reflecting:** No longer fearful of quiet and stillness, I embrace wisdom and choose to reflect on my life and learn from my experiences.

» **Stabilizing:** Avoiding the chaos that accompanies sickness, I choose stability.

» **Learning:** Living beyond immediate urges and impulsive drives, I choose opportunities to learn and grow.

» **Building:** No longer falling apart, I choose to build up others and myself in body, mind, and spirit.

» **Growing:** Tolerating discomfort, I choose to grow in my relationships with God, other people, and myself.

» **Integrating:** No longer accommodating splintered pieces of myself, I choose to integrate all of who I am to become a healthy, whole, and functioning individual.

» **Forgiving:** No longer harboring bitterness and resentment, I choose to freely forgive others.

» **Resolving:** No longer fleeing from conflict or avoiding confrontation, I choose to resolve issues with others to promote peace, reconciliation, and healing.

» **Restoring:** No longer stealing freedom from others or

allowing them to steal mine, I choose to restore what has been lost.

» **Reaching:** No longer waiting for others to notice or validate me, I am reaching out to others in need.

» **Sharing:** No longer hoarding possessions, talent, or time, I choose to share gratefully all that I've been given from God.

» **Serving:** No longer enslaved to serve others under compulsion, I choose to serve with gratitude because God has called me to do it.

» **Giving:** No longer greedily robbing others of their time, confidence, or reputation, I choose to give from the abundance I've been given.

» **Leading:** No longer allowing others to determine my course, I choose to stand up and lead others to a new way of living.

» **Providing:** No longer taking whatever I can get from others, I provide others with time, attention, encouragement, affirmation, and respect.

» **Utilizing:** No longer afraid to ask for help, I reap the benefits of resources that enrich my life.

» **Comforting:** No longer the victim of another's neglect or cruelty, I take time to receive and experience comfort from God, others, and myself.

» **Experiencing:** No longer bullied by distractions and obsessions, I choose to experience being fully present wherever I am.

» **Protecting:** Avoiding dangerous people and places,

I protect the gains I've made by investing in those who help me stay grounded in reality.

» **Persevering:** No longer a victim of my past, I persevere through difficult times to experience the blessings God has for me and for those I love.

Closing Prayer
This week, God, open our eyes to see what is happening inside us, and to notice what is happening around us, as well. With the light of your Spirit, enable us to face the things inside of us that we've avoided or ignored. Embolden us to live lives of faithfulness in our relationships with others, so that every yes or no may be offered with integrity and courage. Amen.

Questions for Personal Reflection

1. In your group time, you began to consider the condition of your heart and the borders you have drawn. Ask the Holy Spirit to open your eyes to the true condition of your heart. Draw a picture of how you see the territory of your heart. Is it too wall-like? Too porous?

Prayerfully offer this snapshot of your heart to God.

2. The first three steps of the Twelve Steps of Life Recovery are meant to ground us in a right relationship with Jesus, our higher power:

> *Step 1: We admitted we were powerless over our problems and that our lives had become unmanageable.*

> *Step 2: We came to believe that a Power greater than ourselves could restore us to sanity.*

> *Step 3: We made a decision to turn our wills and our lives over to the care of God.*

Though some people come to faith when they become keenly aware that their lives have become unmanageable, others—even people of faith—have not yet admitted their powerlessness over their problems and have not yet turned their wills and their lives over to the care of God.

"I HAVE MY ACT TOGETHER."   **"I AM UNDONE."**

←——————————————————————→

On a scale that ranges from "I am running my own life and pretty much have it together" to "I am out of control and have fallen apart," as shown above, where would you place yourself on the spectrum? Answer for three scenarios:

> *F: When you first came to faith*

> *L: When you were at your lowest*

> *T: Where you are today*

Jot down a few specific examples from each period of your life. Those examples will become valuable as you trace the trajectory of your journey to take your life back.

3. Steps 4–7 and Step 10 challenge us to be honest with ourselves about who we really are.

> *Step 4: We made a searching and fearless moral inventory of ourselves.*
>
> *Step 5: We admitted to God, to ourselves, and to another human being the exact nature of our wrongs.*
>
> *Step 6: We were entirely ready to have God remove all these defects of character.*
>
> *Step 7: We humbly asked God to remove our shortcomings.*
>
> *Step 10: We continued to take personal inventory, and when we were wrong, promptly admitted it.*

You've done the hard work of looking at your wounds, and now it's imperative that you also look at where you've failed. Take the time to do a searching and fearless moral inventory of yourself in your journal. This involves peeling away anything that has hidden the truth about who you are and the choices you've made. Focus on where you are today, and be honest about what you identify. When you're done, share your inventory with your safe person.

4. Steps 8 and 9 help us to address our relationships with others.

> *Step 8: We made a list of all persons we had harmed and became willing to make amends to them all.*

> *Step 9: We made direct amends to such people wherever possible, except when to do so would injure them or others.*

Jesus valued making amends so much that he commanded his followers to pursue reconciliation before they offered their gifts to God at the altar. As with all of the Twelve Steps, if we try to skirt around them, we stunt our growth and healing.

If you've sought to make amends with someone, write how you felt before the encounter, during it, and afterward.

Before:

During:

After:

If you haven't yet sought to make amends, describe what you anticipate the experience will be like. Then commit to God your desire to make amends.

5. In Step 11, we journey with Jesus in a way that strengthens us daily.

> *Step 11: We sought through prayer and meditation to improve our conscious contact with God, praying only for knowledge of his will for us and the power to carry it out.*

Identify the time—a season or moment—when you were most aware of your relationship with Jesus. Were there certain practices that you used? Particular studies or guides? Did you set aside a special time or place? Was there a person or group of people who journeyed with you? Jot these down and consider how they might influence your practices today.

6. Step 12 is the final step for a reason. It can be tempting to rush to share the process and avoid doing the work itself. Your sharing will be most meaningful when you can report what God *has done* for you, rather than what God *can do* for someone else.

> *Step 12: Having had a spiritual awakening as the result of these steps, we tried to carry this message to others, and to practice these principles in all our affairs.*

We are all works in process, but it helps to record our victories along the way. Write below what God has done for you so far. Share this progress report with your safe person.

7. Moving forward: Keep practicing the role of *developer* by continuing to ask yourself the question, "*Now* what do I need to do?"

Meditate

In the first group discussion question, how did you depict the perimeter around your heart? Was it impenetrable, keeping all others out? Or was it too flimsy, allowing access to your heart to those who aren't safe?

When you think of a firm but flexible border that allows you to be in relationship with others yet also protects you from harm, what image comes to your mind? Visualize and describe the kind of boundary that allows for both *openness* and *safety*.

When you discover an image that allows you to be in safe, healthy relationships with others, spend time imagining that strong, healthy perimeter as you make it your own.

Focus on Scripture

Confess your sins to each other and pray for each
other so that you may be healed. The earnest prayer
of a righteous person has great power and produces
wonderful results.

JAMES 5:16

This week, make James 5:16 your own: *I will confess my sins to
my safe person—I will pray for him or her, and he or she will pray
for me—so that we both may be healed.*

Start and end each day this week with these words, and seek
to *live them out.*

Take Your Life Back Experiment

You've learned a lot so far about taking your life back, but learning is not enough. The journey to take your life back involves
tearing down walls and replacing them with firm and flexible
borders. Identify a relationship in which you've built a wall that
has separated you from others. Describe how the wall that you
erected for self-protection ended up keeping you bound.

Make a list of people you have walled off in one way or
another. This week, choose one of those people and do some
demolition work on that wall.

The person I've walled off is _____

_____

This week I can _____

_____

After you've taken the first step, jot down some reflections on that experience. How did you feel as you anticipated the encounter?

How did you feel during it?

How did you feel afterward?

Insights
Use this space to jot down any insights that arise during the group discussion or your time of personal reflection.

FINAL ENCOURAGEMENT

YOU'VE DONE THE hard work of looking at the internal and external forces that have had a hold on your life, and at the choices you've made in the wake of your experiences. You now have the tools you need to take your life back so that you can grasp the purpose and meaning you were designed to experience. You are not alone on this journey. We are rooting for you, and God is with you.

We hope and pray that you're as convinced as we are that you were made for so much more than you've experienced. You were made for a life that really is life. Stay the course. Trust God. Persevere, no matter what.

Leader's Guide

THANK YOU FOR leading this group. Your role is to provide a safe space where everyone is valued and respected, and to facilitate the conversation, guiding your group through discussion and prayer. During each session, you'll welcome and encourage the voices of all participants.

If anyone violates the safety of the group—for example, if a participant speaks unkindly to another member or the discussion becomes heated—it's your job to step in to ensure that proper order is restored and that the group experience stays safe for everyone. That doesn't mean you need an advanced counseling degree; it simply means that as the shepherd of the group, your responsibility is to protect the sheep.

Each session begins with a brief welcome video from Stephen Arterburn and David Stoop, which can be found online at www.takeyourlifeback.tv. After the group watches the video, begin the discussion time by reading the opening prayer (or opening with a prayer of your own), having someone read the Scripture focus verses, and then introducing the conversation starter to help people begin to open up. Continue with the group discussion questions, and then wrap up the meeting by reading the closing prayer.

Encourage group members to engage with the personal reflection questions at home. This section gives participants an opportunity to go deeper in their study and to integrate what they're learning by reading *Take Your Life Back* with what they are discovering during the group discussions. This section also encourages quiet meditation and Scripture engagement. Invite group members to share each week the results of their Take Your Life Back Experiment.

Here are some guidelines for group expectations to discuss at the first session:

1. *Attend each session.* Life and schedules can become harried, but we suggest that you ask members to commit to attending each session and alerting the leader in advance if they cannot attend. This consistency benefits both individuals and the group.

2. *Respect every participant.* Offer every participant a listening ear and generous heart. The role of group members is to listen and pray for others in the group, not to offer advice, judgment, or shame. Show other members the respect you'd like to receive.

3. *Keep what's shared within the room.* Emphasize the importance of confidentiality and ask each group member to commit to honoring the trust of other members by not repeating outside of the group any information from group discussions. *If something is shared that indicates that someone inside or outside of the group is in danger, the group leader should*

use wisdom and discretion in following up with the proper authorities.

4. *Extend permission to come as you are.* Everyone is welcome to share, but nobody is obligated. Because we all find ourselves at different places on the journey to take our lives back, some group members may choose to do more listening than talking.

5. *Make space for everyone.* Some participants may be tempted to do more talking than listening. Remind everyone to be aware of the needs of the whole group. If you find that some group members need to share a lot more than others, you may need to encourage them to find another resource, such as a trained therapist, to process their journeys more deeply.

31-Day Guide for Incorporating Truth into Your Daily Life

Use these daily reminders throughout the month as you take your life back.

DAY 1: SEEING
Rejecting distortions and manipulation of the truth, I choose to see others as they really are and to see myself as I really am.

DAY 2: SURRENDERING
Resisting the urge to take control, I choose to surrender to God and his wisdom.

DAY 3: FEELING
Refusing to numb myself, I choose to honor my feelings and what I can learn from them.

DAY 4: BELIEVING
Rejecting crippling doubt, I choose to believe that God is real and that he cares for me.

DAY 5: HEALING
Allowing nothing or no one to take control over me, I surrender to the healing power of the Holy Spirit.

DAY 6: CHOOSING
Refusing to believe the lie that I am stuck forever, I exercise my freedom to choose to *do the next right thing*.

DAY 7: SEARCHING
Rejecting distortion and manipulation, I search for wisdom and truth from God to guide me in all I do.

DAY 8: CONNECTING
Rejecting isolation, detachment, and darkness, I choose to connect with God and others and to walk in the light.

DAY 9: BELONGING
No longer feeling rejected or abandoned, I recognize that I am included. I belong to God and to God's people.

DAY 10: RECEIVING
No longer bound by the demands and neediness of others, I receive from God and from others.

DAY 11: AGREEING
Renouncing half-truths, shame, and toxic distortions of reality, I agree with truth and everything that brings life.

DAY 12: **REFLECTING**
No longer fearful of quiet and stillness, I embrace wisdom and choose to reflect on my life and learn from my experiences.

DAY 13: **STABILIZING**
Avoiding the chaos that accompanies sickness, I choose stability.

DAY 14: **LEARNING**
Living beyond immediate urges and impulsive drives, I choose opportunities to learn and grow.

DAY 15: **BUILDING**
No longer falling apart, I choose to build up others and myself in body, mind, and spirit.

DAY 16: **GROWING**
Tolerating discomfort, I choose to grow in my relationships with God, other people, and myself.

DAY 17: **INTEGRATING**
No longer accommodating splintered pieces of myself, I choose to integrate all of who I am to become a healthy, whole, and functioning individual.

DAY 18: **FORGIVING**
No longer harboring bitterness and resentment, I choose to freely forgive others.

DAY 19: RESOLVING

No longer fleeing from conflict or avoiding confrontation, I choose to resolve issues with others to promote peace, reconciliation, and healing.

DAY 20: RESTORING

No longer stealing freedom from others or allowing them to steal mine, I choose to restore what has been lost.

DAY 21: REACHING

No longer waiting for others to notice or validate me, I am reaching out to others in need.

DAY 22: SHARING

No longer hoarding possessions, talent, or time, I choose to share gratefully all that I've been given from God.

DAY 23: SERVING

No longer enslaved to serve others under compulsion, I choose to serve with gratitude because God has called me to do it.

DAY 24: GIVING

No longer greedily robbing others of their time, confidence, or reputation, I choose to give from the abundance I've been given.

DAY 25: LEADING

No longer allowing others to determine my course, I choose to stand up and lead others to a new way of living.

DAY 26: **PROVIDING**

No longer taking whatever I can get from others, I provide others with time, attention, encouragement, affirmation, and respect.

DAY 27: **UTILIZING**

No longer afraid to ask for help, I reap the benefits of resources that enrich my life.

DAY 28: **COMFORTING**

No longer the victim of another's neglect or cruelty, I take time to receive and experience comfort from God, others, and myself.

DAY 29: **EXPERIENCING**

No longer bullied by distractions and obsessions, I choose to experience being fully present wherever I am.

DAY 30: **PROTECTING**

Avoiding dangerous people and places, I protect the gains I've made by investing in those who help me stay grounded in reality.

DAY 31: **PERSEVERING**

No longer a victim of my past, I persevere through difficult times to experience the blessings God has for me and for those I love.

Resources for Further Discovery and Growth

FIND A SUPPORT GROUP
Find a recovery support group in your area at
http://newlife.com/new-life-groups.

FIND A COUNSELOR
Contact New Life for a confidential, personalized referral:
http://newlife.com/counselors.

MORE RESOURCES ONLINE
Find radio, TV, workshop, and counseling resources online at
http://newlife.com.

BOOKS
Toxic Faith: Experiencing Healing from Painful Spiritual Abuse
by Stephen Arterburn and Jack Felton
Forgiving What You'll Never Forget by David Stoop
Boundaries: When to Say Yes, How to Say No by Dr. Henry
Cloud and Dr. John Townsend

The Twelve Steps of Life Recovery

1. We admitted we were powerless over our problems and that our lives had become unmanageable.

2. We came to believe that a Power greater than ourselves could restore us to sanity.

3. We made a decision to turn our wills and our lives over to the care of God.

4. We made a searching and fearless moral inventory of ourselves.

5. We admitted to God, to ourselves, and to another human being the exact nature of our wrongs.

6. We were entirely ready to have God remove all these defects of character.

7. We humbly asked God to remove our shortcomings.

8. We made a list of all persons we had harmed and became willing to make amends to them all.

9. We made direct amends to such people wherever possible, except when to do so would injure them or others.

10. We continued to take personal inventory, and when we were wrong, promptly admitted it.

11. We sought through prayer and meditation to improve our conscious contact with God, praying only for knowledge of his will for us and the power to carry it out.

12. Having had a spiritual awakening as the result of these steps, we tried to carry this message to others, and to practice these principles in all our affairs.

(The Twelve Steps of Life Recovery have been adapted with permission from the Twelve Steps of Alcoholics Anonymous.)

Notes

1. Cindy Hazan and Phillip Shaver, "Romantic Love Conceptualized as an Attachment Process," *Journal of Personality and Social Psychology* 52, no. 3 (1987): 511–524.
2. Answers:
    - T   I am worthless garbage to be discarded.
    - G   I shouldn't have left my wife and kids.
    - T   I'm not worth loving.
    - G   I feel guilty for hitting my wife.
    - T   I'm not worth showing up for.
    - G   I shouldn't be cheating on my husband.
    - T   I'm not worth protecting.
    - G   I feel awful for lying to my parents.
    - T   I'm not worth sticking around for.
    - G   I'm mortified that I got drunk last night.

About the Authors

Stephen Arterburn, M.Ed., is the founder and chairman of New Life Ministries—the nation's largest faith-based broadcast, counseling, and treatment ministry. He is also the host of the nationally syndicated *New Life Live!* daily radio program, which airs on more than 180 radio stations nationwide, on Sirius XM radio, and on television. Steve is the founder of the Women of Faith conferences, attended by more than five million women. A nationally known public speaker, Steve has been featured in national media venues such as *Oprah*, *ABC World News Tonight*, *Good Morning America*, *CNN Live*, the *New York Times*, *USA Today*, *US News & World Report*, and *Rolling Stone*. In August 2000, Steve was inducted into the National Speakers Association's Hall of Fame. A bestselling author, Steve has more than ten million books in print, including the popular Every Man's Battle series. He is a multiple Gold Medallion–winning author and has been nominated for numerous other writing awards. He is also an award-winning study Bible editor of ten projects, including the *Life Recovery Bible*.

Steve has degrees from Baylor University and the University of North Texas, as well as two honorary doctorates. He resides with his family in Indiana.

David Stoop, Ph.D, is a licensed clinical psychologist in California. He received a master's in theology from Fuller Theological Seminary and a doctorate from the University of Southern California. He is frequently heard as a cohost on the nationally syndicated *New Life Live!* radio and TV program. David is the founder and director of the Center for Family Therapy in Newport Beach, California. He is also an adjunct professor at Fuller Seminary and serves on the executive board of the American Association of Christian Counselors. David is a Gold Medallion–winning author who has written more than thirty books, including *Forgiving What You'll Never Forget* and *Rethink How You Think*. He resides with his wife, Jan, in Newport Beach, California, and they have three sons and six grandchildren.

Margot Starbuck is a speaker, columnist, author, and collaborative writer. A graduate of Princeton Seminary and Westmont College, she is passionate about effective communication and about equipping folks to love our (sometimes unlikely or overlooked) neighbors.

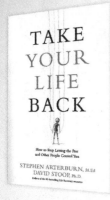

TAKE YOUR LIFE BACK

A New Life Intensive Workshop

Speakers:
Steve Arterburn
and
Dave Stoop

So what's the next right step? Even when you want a life of wholeness, health, and fulfillment, the journey can be filled with painful turns and surprising twists, and it can lead to isolation. But the path toward wholeness is never one you have to walk alone!

Join Steve and Dave at the *Take Your Life Back Intensive Workshop*, where they share more than 8 hours of biblical truths and life-changing information on topics such as "Discovering Who or What Owns You" and "Surviving Broken Connection." A New Life Network Counselor, in small group sessions, will help you process what you have learned and develop a specific and personal plan for your daily life. A plan that, if followed, reveals God's faithfulness in your everyday life, enriches your life and relationships like never before, and gives you the strength and freedom to *Take Your Life Back!*

For information on workshops or to register, call
800-NEW-LIFE (639-5433)
newlife.com

CP1154

FIND HEALING IN GOD'S WORD EVERY DAY.

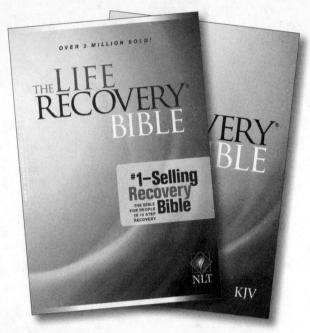

Celebrating over 2 million copies sold!

The Life Recovery Bible is today's bestselling Bible for people in recovery. In the accurate and easy-to-understand New Living Translation, *The Life Recovery Bible* leads people to the true source of healing—God himself. Special features created by two of today's leading recovery experts—David Stoop, Ph.D., and Stephen Arterburn, M.Ed.—include the following:

Recovery Study Notes: Thousands of Recovery-themed notes interspersed throughout the Bible pinpoint passages and thoughts important to recovery.

Twelve Step Devotionals: A reading chain of 84 Bible-based devotionals tied to the Twelve Steps of recovery.

Serenity Prayer Devotionals: Based on the Serenity Prayer, these 29 devotionals are placed next to the verses from which they are drawn.

Recovery Principle Devotionals: Bible-based devotionals, arranged topically, are a guide to key recovery principles.

Find *The Life Recovery Bible* at your local Christian bookstore or wherever books are sold. Learn more at www.LifeRecoveryBible.com.

Available editions:
NLT Hardcover 978-1-4143-0962-0
NLT Softcover 978-1-4143-0961-3
Personal Size Softcover 978-1-4143-1626-0
Large Print Hardcover 978-1-4143-9856-3

Large Print Softcover 978-1-4143-9857-0
KJV Hardcover 978-1-4143-8150-3
KJV Softcover 978-1-4143-8506-8

CP0107